Jennifer Gordon

Poems To Read In The Rain

Jennifer Gordon

"Jennifer's poetry whispers both sweet and sour truths in your ear and connects you both to yourself and the wider world through its rich imagery and powerful storytelling. To read her poetry is to live many lives in a few breaths."
- Mythos Poets Society

Poems To Read In The Rain

Jennifer Gordon

Poems To Read In The Rain

Jennifer Gordon

Curious Corvid Publishing, LLC
Ohio

Poems To Read In The Rain

Poems To Read In The Rain by Jennifer Gordon

Published by Curious Corvid Publishing, LLC.

Copyright © 2021 by Jennifer Gordon

All rights reserved. Published in the United States by Curious Corvid Publishing, LLC, Ohio. No portion of this book may be reproduced in any form without permission from the publisher, except as permitted by U.S. copyright law.

Cover design by Ravven White
Edited by Enoch Black
Photo by MAD Five O Photography
Interior photos licensed through Shutterstock

Printed in the United States of America
Cataloging-in-Publication Data is on file with the Library of Congress.
ISBN: 978-1-7368675-6-3
ISBN (ebook): 978-1-7368675-7-0
www.curiouscorvidpublishing.com

Jennifer Gordon

I would like to express an immense amount of gratitude for my husband, Matt. He has loved me hardest when I am at my worst. He is the strongest man I know.

I am also incredibly grateful for my friends Enoch Black, Joanna Morey, and Alex Martinez, who selflessly dedicated their time to helping me organize and edit this collection.

Poems To Read In The Rain

You can find more of Jennifer's poetry on Instagram
@jennifergordonpoetry

Jennifer Gordon

Chapter One:
Love and Things Like It

Poems To Read In The Rain

Jennifer Gordon

Each of us has our lot in life
I am the observer, the humble weed
The poet, silently planting seeds
Of words that spring up from the dirt
Entangle my roots with written truths
And drain my form until I thirst
For one more glimpse of you, my muse
The one who waters lonely hours
With drips of moments my soul devours
You are the moonlight gracing petals
In a midnight garden of growth unsettled

Poems To Read In The Rain

I believe if I gave you all that I had
Offered the things you claim to need
You would hold them lightly in your hands
And in time, you would turn from me
Begin to wander through the trees
In search of something, anything
Just a little bit more interesting to hold
And so, I will keep my heart within my ribs
Protecting the pieces I wish I could give

There once was a girl
Who fell in love with the stars
She wrote love letters
As the years went by
Heartfelt notes
She released to the night
Although her words
Were never returned
She found peace in knowing
Her thoughts were heard
She loved the stars
Till the day she died
And they burned for her
In a silent sky

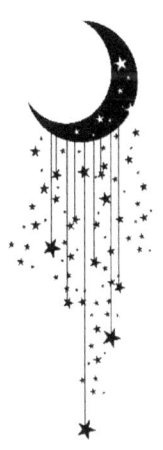

Love.
The raw ache of desire
Mounting in your chest
The sickness in your stomach
After a sleepless night's unrest
The tangled vines
Wrapping abundantly
Around your brittle bones
Tying knots
In the chambers of your heart,
Felt by you alone
A fire burning in the night,
Immune to efforts of suppression
No form of will nor logic
Holding power
To subdue its obsession
At long last,
It is the ever heated embers
The warmth running daily
Through your veins
The swell
Of everything you can't explain

Jennifer Gordon

She will ever be the color red
For the passion flowing through her veins
And the blood of a thousand broken hearts
Beautifully stained upon her hands

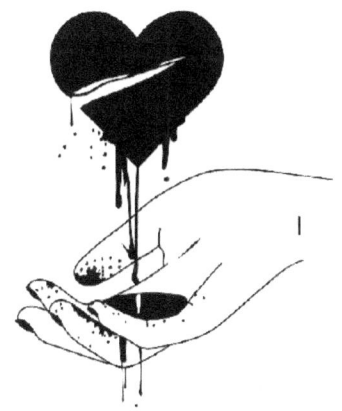

Poems To Read In The Rain

She was the ink that formed his poems
Crafted from pieces of broken molds
She was the muse who wrote the songs
His soul had listened for all along
She was the name upon his tongue
The breath of contentment in his lungs
She was the way, the taste he craved
The creature by whom his life was saved

They say that love is free of pain
but they must be referring
to a woman who's been tamed

Poems To Read In The Rain

Lust resides in a cage made of string
Perched inside like an innocent thing
Disguised in layers of plume and crown
Singing along with a careless crowd
Observing mindless passersby
Caressing thoughts from wandering eyes
Awaiting the moment they feel at ease
Casually spreading seductive wings
Out she slips from between the threads
Stirring flesh and turning heads

Jennifer Gordon

All at once
I knew too much
Of desires born
From a single touch

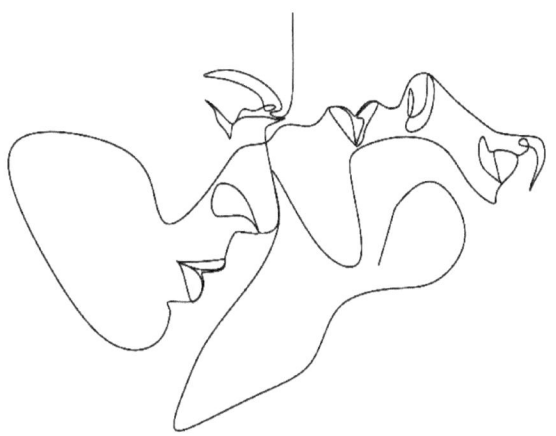

Poems To Read In The Rain

All it took was my palm upon your chest
For a fraction of a moment I forgot who I was
Suddenly I was dreaming of losing myself
The risks I would take to be in your hands
The inevitable fall and where I might land
The scars I would bear to shield your sins
The heart I would lose to let you in

She fell so fast
In an instant
Off the ledge
Free falling
Heart longing
For something
She knew she
Would one day
Be mourning

Poems To Read In The Rain

I was taught all lessons in black and white
Right and wrong, now or never, do or die
Live by the rules, for they keep you safe
In my ignorance, I failed to see
The beauty behind the lies
The abundant hues of gray
But now, I know the role exceptions play
For there are a thousand shadows in your eyes
And they are all I want to see

Jennifer Gordon

Pull me close and catch my breath
Let it weave around your neck
Breathe me in, full and deep
Through your lungs, let it seep
Down into your lovely bones
As fragments of my scent
Tangle with your own

Poems To Read In The Rain

Such sweet surrender
As walls of my soul begin to quake
Weak at the knees as boundaries break
Tumbling down in knots unwound
Cascades of trembling, wordless sounds
Plunge me into your open sea
Let it capture the breathless mess I am
The taste of salt upon my tongue
Whispered yearnings for pleasures unsung
Hold me here in steaming waters
My curves seek shelter upon your skin
Silkened sheets caressing limbs
Drown me in this love untamed
So I may sink in supple waves
Of blissful touch and spinal arch
Lost to the night my pulse will flee
Dripping with beads of ecstasy

Fingertips, soft as feathers
Caressing flesh along my spine
Rippled pleasures
Hidden treasures
Breathless cries
Of collisions divine

Poems To Read In The Rain

I have never felt more beautiful
Than the very first time I saw your face
As you watched me enter the room
And from that moment I knew
That the beatings of my swelling heart
Would always and only belong to you

Jennifer Gordon

Even the blackest of nights
With constellations adorning the sky
Will never compare to the canvas of your skin
With freckles forming patterns
My fingertips long to follow

Poems To Read In The Rain

Lay me down on our favorite rug
Warm to the touch from the autumn sun
Hold me close, breathe me in
I'll press my lips into your skin
Taste the salt of your collarbone
Savor the way you smell like home

Jennifer Gordon

Come, find comfort in my arms
Sink into my skin and fall apart
My hands are not fragile
They can bear the weight
Of a man unraveled
So lay your head upon my chest
And let me handle all the rest

Poems To Read In The Rain

Hold me close and love me well
For souls like ours can never tell
What is pain and what is bliss
Perhaps in a love this profound
There simply is no difference

Jennifer Gordon

Perhaps the mirror
Only reveals
The flaws your insecurities feel
But to me, my love
You are an immaculate reflection
Of all that heals

Poems To Read In The Rain

They say that beauty is only skin deep
But they don't know you
Or the gardens you keep
How the richness of your soul
Is always in bloom
Nourishing light as it filters through
Or how your magic has its roots
In the words that anchor
Me to you

Jennifer Gordon

Come to me with everything
Pour your soul, empty its caverns
Let my love become your lantern
Take a sigh of deep relief
I'll pocket your heart,
For I am a thief
Of all you treasure deep inside
Please don't bother
There is nowhere to hide
I'll own it all, swallow it down
Let your words become my crown
Follow me, wherever I go
Tracking footprints in the snow

Poems To Read In The Rain

Show me
Your hidden scars
Whisper the words
That make you ache
Place my hands
In empty spaces
Tell me all
The ways to go
About beginning
To make you whole

Jennifer Gordon

Lean on me
Not as a crutch
But as the one who remains
When others run

Poems To Read In The Rain

To me, my love, you are weightless
A burden I am glad to bear
Essential as the evening air

She is the sun
The only source of light upon my soul
My warmth, my blood, my every breath
Is anchored to her core

Poems To Read In The Rain

You are the sun to the moon of my heart
For I have always been at home in the dark
But in my soul, a beauty blooms
When touched by the light that shines from you

Jennifer Gordon

When love comes home
You feel her there
Deep in the marrow of your bones

Poems To Read In The Rain

Your faults cause waves
Amidst the sea
Your mistakes may never
Be washed away
Still, you are the bravest thing
I've ever seen

Jennifer Gordon

When I was caught
Up in the storm
You were the coat
That kept me warm

Poems To Read In The Rain

And if it comes to pass
That the pouring of myself for you
Claims even the deepest of my breaths
If I am drained of all I can give
Weary and withered beneath the stars
Having spent the moments meant to be mine
On giving myself to the wonder you are
Then I will rest in sweet release
For deep in the corners of my heart
This love for you is all I need

Jennifer Gordon

For you
I would set my heart on fire
Suffer as it burned
Reduced to blackened ashes
Secretly
I would add them to your tea
Pray
That they would make their way
Deep into your flowing veins
Settling
At last to rest
In the delicate spaces of your chest

Poems To Read In The Rain

Is it strange to envy the walls of your home?
The structure and marrow that form your bones?
Is it wrong to long to be the songs
That ease your spirit and keep you calm?
Or what of the shelter you find in the trees
When you face an unrelenting breeze?

I wonder where your refuge lies
In the moments when no one is by your side
As long as you are in this world
My heart will ache to be the one
Who claims within you a sacred space
And dwells in the things that keep you safe

He was built of flames
Instantly ignited
But gone with the rain
She was the coal
Burning low
Holding on to dying light

Poems To Read In The Rain

Last night I embroidered your name on my heart
I gasped at the pain, shook as I worked
But such is the way with passionate art

Jennifer Gordon

Loving you was like
Being caught in the rain
Invigorating, breathtaking
Leaving me chilled to the bone

Poems To Read In The Rain

I have a request
Would you sit with me?
I think your presence is all I need
We don't need to touch, or even speak
Is that allowed, is that a thing?
Just our two souls, alone in one space
Knowing our silent breaths interlace

I am the rocks of the ocean floor
Deeply rooted and beautifully worn
You are the light that calls to my heart
A wondrous pattern of evening stars
I was held by the depths
As you were swept to the sky
But even the heavens are not too high
Even this distance is not too far
To keep me from yearning
For all that you are

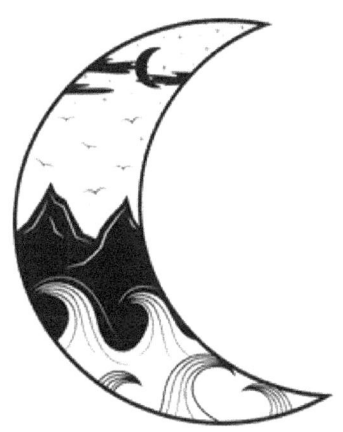

Poems To Read In The Rain

I no longer
Believe in love
But that one word
Is all I have left
Of you, of us
Of all the moments
We have lost

Beautiful soul,
You carved this valley
In my chest
Hacked my walls apart
Until nothing was left
Yet the pattern made
By scattered fragments
Of my heart
Remains my favorite
Work of art

Poems To Read In The Rain

You may say that I'm regrettable
Let's be honest, it's probably true
But please, whatever you do
Don't call me forgettable
And I shall vow the same for you

Perhaps in our next life,
I will be the twigs
And you shall be the string
So the birds we love
May build their homes
From the bones we used to be

Poems To Read In The Rain

You ask if I ever think of you
"Ever"
Such an absurd little word
As if my heart knew how to beat
To any rhythm besides your name

Jennifer Gordon

If it should come to pass,
That I am the first to be claimed by death
Then I shall insist that my body be burned
Reduced to ashes of lessons learned
I will beg my loved ones to cast me out
Amidst a storm of roaring wind
So my remnants may travel to the ends of the earth
In search of the man for whom I yearn
And settle there upon your warmth
My flesh shall seek its final rest
Burrowed within your weathered skin
And I am sure, by the time they bind
The ghost of my soul will have found your home
So your oldest years may at last be spent
In the presence of a love I have longed to give
To shower upon you while I lived
But in death I shall haunt your every breath
So you may be filled with all that I am

Poems To Read In The Rain

If you are to be the death of me
Please, kill me slowly
Let me savor the agony of your touch
Drenched in sorrow, heart undone
Break me apart in a million moments
So that with my final breaths,
At least I may die a poet

Chapter 2: Grief Is a Grave On An Open Road

Poems To Read In The Rain

Jennifer Gordon

The world may be more than I can bear
I always seem to fall apart
These days there are fires everywhere
And I was born with a paper heart

Poems To Read In The Rain

Tenderly, I wrap forsaken thoughts
In layers of earth and tainted cloth
Press my palms upon their fate
Holding misery as it shakes
Rattled nerves and scorching shame
Whispered waves to drown the pain
Where in this pit is the flare for rescue?
Where is the map to hunt and reach you?
Tangled in a web of threads
Woven by venom and talking heads
Just leave me here, turn and run
Deserted by grace and the lies on their tongues
My hands are full of words to be spun
But my grave shall simply read "undone"

Jennifer Gordon

Let me sleep
Barely breathing
Cocooned in cotton sheets
Wake me years from now
When his taste is no longer in my mouth
And I can't recall what love was about
When the grief has faded from my veins
Once time has had its way with pain
Wake me when the shaking stops
When the walls are built
And my heart is numb

Poems To Read In The Rain

So this is how it feels
For the spirit to die
While the rest of the body
Is still alive

Jennifer Gordon

If sadness was an ocean
I'd be buried in the sea
A lonely pile of bones
Washed bare by the salt of time

Poems To Read In The Rain

Your absence has broken more than my heart
It has punctured my lungs and stolen my spirit
Weakened my flesh and stripped my esteem
I tread through water with limbs that are heavy
From the weight of your words embedded in my skin
Anchored to your ghost, by chains I cannot break
For they are darkened, invisible things, taunting me
Drawing drips of blood that no one else can see
This ever present night feels void of even the moon
No end in sight as time grows cold
I have always prided myself on my own strength
And yet, here I am, with waves of heartache
Rolling over my ruins in broken rhythm
Drowning in an endless sea
Clinging to a fading hope
That the shore will save what's left of me

Jennifer Gordon

You have ruined more than just these moments
You have damned the road ahead
For my heart has taken all that it can
And the precious pieces that are left
Are burned and branded by your hands

Poems To Read In The Rain

I should be strong enough to save myself
To follow the voice of my own advice
But the surface of sanity sears my skin
Revolts in my lungs as I breathe it in
The brick of your name
Is a weight my bones have claimed
And it will surely be upon my lips
As I slip upon unstable ground
Sinking farther down
For even in these shallow waters
A heavy heart can drown

Jennifer Gordon

On my worst nights
When my hands are shaking
Limbs still unsteady from the fall
When loss is around my throat
And I feel like grief is all I know
I drag myself down to the shore
Write your name there in the sand
Just to feel a part of you in my hands

Poems To Read In The Rain

I build bouquets of broken things
Like brittle hopes and long held dreams
And thoughts that you had once loved me

Jennifer Gordon

My dreams have been bled dry
Slowly seeping from my eyes
Salt and blood, hopeless screams
Silenced by the passing time

Poems To Read In The Rain

I had a dream that I could scream
Into the chaos of the wind
And the streams of power rushing by
Would carry shallow, desperate cries
Away to a town where you could be found
And there they would whisper in your ear
Beg your ribs to be let in
Reminding you of what had been

Jennifer Gordon

It's not that I want to die
It's just that I'm so damn tired
Of trying to feel alive

Poems To Read In The Rain

I fade back
Into the shadows
Praying the darkness is enough
To swallow me whole
Perhaps I am desperate enough
To simply disappear

Jennifer Gordon

In time
He resolved himself to sadness
To be gentle with his heart
For it felt like shaking shattered glass
Each and every time he laughed

Poems To Read In The Rain

Way back there, swallowed by shadows
Deep in the darkest corner of the room
Behind the rusted, overplayed thoughts
And webs of woven partial truths
Is the glimmer of a man who used to be you

Somewhere on the road
Between regret and grief
Is the vision of a girl
Who used to be me

Poems To Read In The Rain

Words like burns, coat thick within my throat
Lumped into lesions, pricks of sorrow
Memories of wasted tomorrows
Yesterdays that came and went
Cries compiled but never spent
So many things I have longed to say
Burdens I have yearned to cast away
A hundred things I wish I had said
Maybe more
Maybe if I started now,
My thoughts would gather as grains of sand
Ample enough to form a shore
Where I could lay my body down
Bent and broken on reflections profound
Meet me there beneath the moon
Let me scream this fire from my wounds

Jennifer Gordon

Some nights I fear my ribs will break
While being crushed beneath the weight
From piles heaped upon my chest
Of words I felt and never said

Poems To Read In The Rain

I lay awake on full moon nights
Fearing the fallout of my failures
My frail inability to remove
These promises from my lips
To strip my limbs of the warmth
From your hands
To swallow the vows I spoke out loud
To take them back, make my heart retract
Yet somehow still leave my soul intact

Jennifer Gordon

Sometimes I forget that my heart is broken
A sliver of a dream, for only a moment

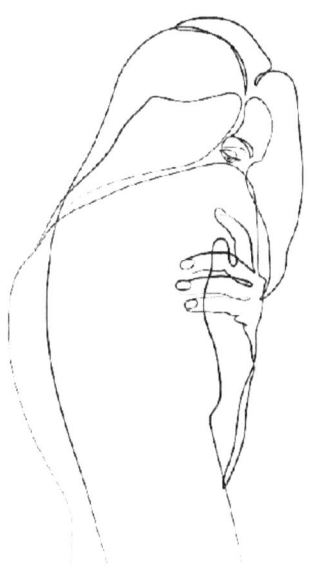

Poems To Read In The Rain

Anguish comes in bitter waves
Sorrow floats in shadows
But you,
You hover like a mist above the sea
A constant presence in the air
I beg the winds of time to blow
To push you farther out to sea
Please
Drift away and let me be

Jennifer Gordon

Some mornings my hands are shaking
Too much to even lift a pen
To express the dreams I've had
Of waking up beside your warmth
In a world where you had put me first

Poems To Read In The Rain

Where they see a woman, I see a shell
An outer layer of my former self
Merely the cover of a once loved book
Emptied of the pages you took

Today was heavy
Today was unkind
Today I wished
To be somewhere
Anywhere
Other than in
My own mind

Poems To Read In The Rain

They like to ask if I am better yet
If I have managed to forget
As if the trauma hasn't carved a home
Into the structure of my bones
As if I carry a shred of doubt
That I lack the tools to dig it out
They like to ask if time has cured me
If I have finally broken free
As if I still hold onto hope
That the years will grant me ways to cope
As if my heart could detach from the pain
From the burns that are flowing through my veins

Jennifer Gordon

There is a certain kind of pain
That comes from being used
A deeper burn, originating
From the center of your being
Radiating out through flesh and bone
Scorching the mind's eye
Leaving its victim blind
To the truth of their own self worth
Healing comes especially slow
To a broken soul
For there is nothing worse
Than being left with the impression
You were nothing but a stepping stone

Poems To Read In The Rain

Lately, my light feels dim
Depression breeds indifference
Mindlessly settled on my skin
An invisible cloak of apathy
Over shoulders already shaken
How long must I fail in finding freedom
From moments drenched in sadness
Before the demons closing in
Pirate my bones and pull me home

I imagine my sadness
As a weighted blanket
Draped over every inch of skin
Hugging my curves, drawing me in
Pressing down on every pore
Touching every atom of my being
From surface level jaded smile
Down to the depths of my core

Poems To Read In The Rain

Depression is a silent thief
Quietly coming in the night
Invading sleeping hearts
And raiding them of light

Darkness used to feel
Like a lair where demons would hide
Coming out, into the night
Creeping up, along my sides
My hole, my hell
The place anxiety resides
But now it has changed
Into something softer
An empathetic voice
Calling me by name
A place I'd like to crawl inside
Rest my head
Curl into a ball and cry

Poems To Read In The Rain

Depression is a dreadful beast
A creature born in lowly tides
Surfacing to roam through space and time
You never know how long he'll stay
He comes and goes in ghostly ways

In darkness he crawls into your bed,
Burrows deep inside your head
Fills your lungs with weighted breaths
Sinks his teeth into your flesh

Perhaps tonight he'll make his home
In every inch of fragile skin
Peeling your layers down to the bone
Feeding on fear and secret sins

Perhaps tomorrow he'll lay his fur
Thick upon your mouth
Muffling any pitiful words
You had thought of uttering for help

Then he will hide, slink away
Taking rest on a beautiful day
The sun will kiss your shadowed face
For a moment, you may believe you're safe

But he is a tease, this merciless beast
He merely pauses for some sleep
Here he comes, crawling back
Hungry for a midnight snack

Jennifer Gordon

Time is a tease
A manipulative mastermind
The most patient of demons
Pretending to heal us

Poems To Read In The Rain

The hardest form of grief
Is the kind you must conceal
Buried deep within your chest
So those you love can heal

Jennifer Gordon

In the dead of night
It came to me
That poems are symptoms
Of disease
Dripping from the tongue
As untreated wounds
Fester and bleed

Poems To Read In The Rain

Silence settles upon her tongue
Seeps and spreads into her blood
Coats and covers open wounds
Concealing the depth of emotional tombs

Jennifer Gordon

I no longer believe in love stories
Nor fairytales, or wishing stars
I am not interested in cliche lines
And plastered smiles
Do not encourage me
To follow broken childhood dreams
I refuse to place my hope
In fates I cannot foresee
We do not all make it in the end
Things do not always work out for the best
My jaded mind does not miss these things
These little lies I used to believe
In truth, all I ever wanted
To believe in was you
Your love is the only lie I grieve

Poems To Read In The Rain

I do not fear dying
Only living
For there is no hope
In a dead man's bones
And hope is determined
To torment my soul

He has spent years trying to reclaim his heart
To pull it out of her hands, prying apart his ribs
And begging the remains to climb back in
But the human heart has a will of its own
And in time he must accept, that the one
She took from him is never coming back
It seems that all the love he had
Will always and only belong to her
So now he must begin to learn
What else of himself he can give to the world
How he can live as this shell of a man
How he can breathe from a chest that is hollow
And (hardest of all), how to accept
That it will always be the same tomorrow

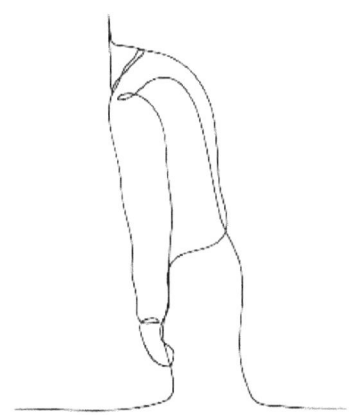

Poems To Read In The Rain

Silence is a language
I never learned to read

Maybe all we really need
Is a few unfiltered moments to scream

Poems To Read In The Rain

I read somewhere today
That grief settles into our DNA
Seeps into the core of who we are
Changes the structure of our hearts
And all of a sudden, I understood
Why the woman I was had not returned
And that perhaps, she never would

Jennifer Gordon

An empty field of forgotten land
Once well loved by weathered hands
Often under troubled skies
I stumble my way here again
Body splayed upon the dirt
Open palms, softened limbs
Feeling grass grazing skin
Here I pray to touch your ghost
Hear your voice, breathe your scent
Something, anything, heaven sent
Void and broken, most nights I stay
Though once in a while
Wearily, mercy comes my way
She throws to me a shooting star
To remind my sorrow where you are

Poems To Read In The Rain

They say to be brave and let love in
But shrapnels of you are still in my skin
And I'm not sure my soul could survive this again

Jennifer Gordon

I want to believe in the words you say
But the world has taught me to be afraid
Of the heartache hiding in good intentions
Of the temporary nature of spoken promises
I want to believe there is truth in your eyes
But my heart has learned of the ways men lie
Of deception designed to fill empty spaces
Of warmth in the illusion of safer havens
I want to embrace the swelling in my chest
But grief reminds me of the lovers who left
And the ache in my ribs after all this time
Tells me to keep my heart confined

Poems To Read In The Rain

My heart was a puzzle of a thousand parts
Dropped on the rocks by careless hands
Scattered by the wind as grains of sand
Where they took rest, I may never know
But I pray for the day
They each make their way home

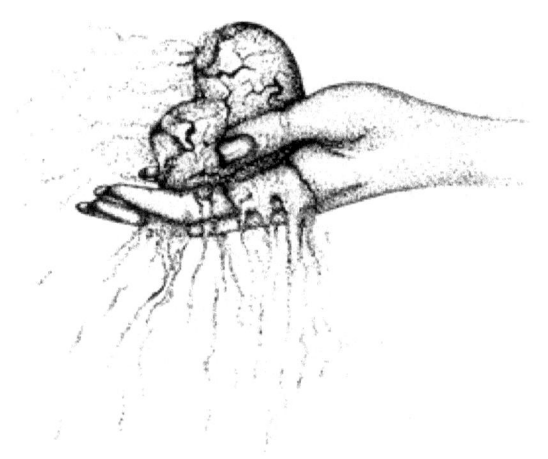

Jennifer Gordon

I will dig these wounds out of my bones
Leave them here beneath the moon
Let the present darkness feast
Upon these symptoms of disease
Guard empty spaces in the night
And await the cure of morning's light

Poems To Read In The Rain

Tonight I carved a grave for you
Deep in the layers of my soul
At the end of me where no one goes
I placed you in and sewed it shut
A final act of forsaken love
The blood beneath my flesh
Will water what is left
Of weakened heart and tired bones
Now I shall wait and observe the seams
To see what next may grow

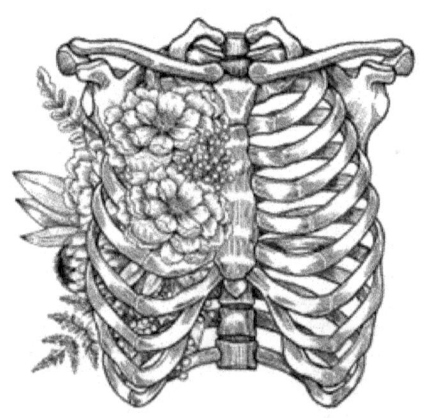

Jennifer Gordon

Chapter 3:
Digging Through the Dirt

Poems To Read In The Rain

Jennifer Gordon

No one is born a poet
We are made by the brutal sands of time
Translating trauma through lyrical rhyme
We are dragged through the pits of hell
Collecting stories we'll bravely tell
We are beaten down by the hands that hold us
Dipping our pens in blue black bruises
We are crushed beneath judgmental stones
Finding strength through words alone
We are mourners in anguish on our lovers' graves
Blooming as artists, watered by pain
We are drowned in the depths of the churning sea
Emerging as mermaids dripping ink
We are the shipwrecked who survived the storm
We are the victims who've been transformed
We are the ordinary, turned heroic
We are muses, we are power, we are poets

Poems To Read In The Rain

I will not slip beneath the surface
Will not succumb to waves of sadness
That wash upon my trembling lips
Dripping salt on labored breaths
Weakened bones and weary heart
Will tread through waters in the dark
For I am a muse to those who weep
And I will prove we can conquer the sea

Jennifer Gordon

In honor of this pain
I will vow to find my way
I will drag myself along the dirt
Learn to walk amidst the hurt
And I will rejoice with every step
Knowing I still have courage left

Poems To Read In The Rain

When a part of yourself is dead and gone
Be patient with the pieces that remain
Training your lungs to breathe again
Is not as easy as it seems

In time, I believe
That wounds sprout wings
So you can rise above
The things you grieve

Poems To Read In The Rain

All I want to do is write
Feel pages at my fingertips
Stain my skin with blackened ink
Breathe the scent of burning paper
As my words turn into smoke
Killing these journals softly
In hopes of saving my own life

Jennifer Gordon

My soul was formed from a broken mold
With bones too sharp for a heart this bold
My tongue was torn from its truth untold
By a world that cares too much for control
My flesh was raked upon the coals
For hints of skin I did not withhold
And I was crushed beneath their stones
Buried in judgment disguised as gold
Now I travel on darkened roads
Collecting shards of myself unknown
And so my dear, you are safer alone
As I am far too jagged for you to hold

Poems To Read In The Rain

I hand sew seams on broken things
Like soulful dreams and self esteem
So I can heal with well loved scars
Remembering how I've come this far

Jennifer Gordon

Despite the fight with grief and pain
I aim to live with no regrets
There is always something to be gained
From the moments in life we cannot forget

Poems To Read In The Rain

I will refuse to fade away
Even if no one asks me to stay

Jennifer Gordon

Amidst the struggle I discovered
You are far less likely to drown
Once removing the weight
Of the world from your shoulders

Poems To Read In The Rain

I am always yearning for deeper roots
Trying to force my growth into familiar soil
Digging my hands into the sand
Gripping tighter at the ground beneath my bones
They say I should plant my feet in one place
Anchor my arms to the walls of my home
And so I cling to what I'm told
Bending and breaking to fit their mold
But advice from good souls can still be wrong
And after all this time, I'm beginning to find
Some of us simply aren't designed
To stay inside the lines
So maybe these roots I've been dying to grow
Have never really been there at all
Maybe the only growth I need
Is the knowledge of who I am meant to be

Jennifer Gordon

Safe in the dark, beneath muted stars
She opened her palms, relieved heavy hands
Of fears long held in stubborn fists
Releasing them quietly to the wind

Fear not, my love
One day
That wicked scar upon your heart
Will boast its brilliance to the world
As your most exquisite work of art

Jennifer Gordon

Dig deeper, my friend
Take rest when you are weary
But never cease your quest
There is strength left
In this well of yours
Floating upon a rising swell
Of all that begs to be expressed
Take your time, let it rise
Embrace the depth of who you are
Let it out and let them hear
A voice that roars in spite of fear

Poems To Read In The Rain

Breathe, my dear
You are allowed to fear
To pulse and swell
To feel the rushing tide
But remember who you are
A siren made to tame the waves
A beacon in the storm
They may fight to hold you down
Steal your breath and hide your voice
But you, my love, will never drown

Jennifer Gordon

Perhaps in the moments we fall apart
We discover the pieces of who we are

Poems To Read In The Rain

I have always hated the color white
The cold blankness of its nature
Void of vibrance and dry of color
A symbol of innocence
What a strange thing to represent
As if any of us can truly comprehend
The meaning of an innocent life

But blackness…now there is beauty
Endless shades of shadows made
Darkness that shelters secrets and lovers
Seductive lace where fingers trace
Coats of panthers and vultures' feathers
A canvas behind the moon as she shines
For black is designed for bodies divine

Perhaps I am drawn to the color of night
Simply because my soul relates
I dream in darkness and paint with grays
Always longing for darker shades
At midnight my sleepless voice comes alive
The songs I sing beg wolves to reply
For they are fierce and so am I

Jennifer Gordon

Forgiveness is not
For the peaceful ones
It is for the warriors
The ones who fight like hell
To rise above

Poems To Read In The Rain

Somewhere along this bitter line
I stepped aside and let anger pass
He rushed on by with a crooked stride
In time reduced to a speck on the path

Last night I dreamt
Of myself as the moon
What a feeling it was
To be on display
How odd to be seen
Only in portions
The rest of me hidden away
Although I suppose
My life is the same
The dark side of the moon
Is never seen
Neither are the secrets in me

Poems To Read In The Rain

If darkness is home
To souls who roam
Then I am a child
Of the night
Thriving amidst
The absence of light

I wish we could all stop measuring
Our worth on broken scales
Self esteem is a fragile thing
Why do we insist
On continuing to place its weight
On shallow illusions fated to break?
We heap and pile our qualities for miles
Lump them together into something
We believe to be worthwhile
Hope and pray they are enough
To tip a dysfunctional unit of measure
A few more notches in the right direction
If only we remembered
The things we used to treasure
Before the world took hold of our throats
Feeding us fiction of what we should be
Placing temptations on our tongues
Wetting a thirst for dreams that are cursed
If only we could all break free
Dig down to our roots
And see the beauty in their growth
Hold our own hearts with gentle hands
With intentions that had learned to understand
That we are more than the sum of our parts
Perhaps we would cease to fall apart
To lose ourselves while chasing stars

Poems To Read In The Rain

I am not the sum of surfaces you see
Not the rumors you hear
Nor the things you assume
I am a dance of working parts
An endless array of fevered thoughts
Flesh and bone, built as a fragile cage
Around a fiercely beating heart

Jennifer Gordon

I have always had a difficult time
Verbally expressing
The heaviness in my mind
I tend to go quiet
When asked to speak my heart
As if I'm doing the words a favor
By keeping them inside
I let them sit beneath my tongue
Sheltered in silence
As if I'm saving them the trauma
Of being misunderstood

Poems To Read In The Rain

I was born with a restless soul
One that wanders,
One that yearns
Traveling unfamiliar roads
Marveling
At the way life twists and turns

Jennifer Gordon

My quest for purpose has taken a turn
I have ceased my search of well traveled places
Instead looking inward at guarded spaces

Poems To Read In The Rain

There is always a silver lining
Some moments will leave it shining
Bright as the stars in a midnight sky
Announcing names, drawing eyes
But, most often I have found
It presents itself in muted tones
When other sounds have filled the room
From the back it plays a humble tune
Unassuming, low and plain
Only heard as notes of grey

Jennifer Gordon

Believe in yourself
Always
For anything less
Is self destruction

Poems To Read In The Rain

She wore her words
And wore them well
As stains on her sleeves
On tattered wings
And dripping from her tongue

Jennifer Gordon

My soul will never be found in the shallows
For I am a swimmer of ocean caves
A freedom seeker who rides the waves
Diving off from the highest cliff
Plunging down into the abyss

Poems To Read In The Rain

Society says that we must choose
But I know this deception to be untrue
We need not declare either hero or villain
Need not label our wild women
In humility
I stand up straight to announce my claim
That both flow freely through my veins

Jennifer Gordon

The fairytale princess has always bored me
If only a dragon could get all the glory
A monster who soars and bares her teeth
Makes a far better muse than a maiden who weeps

Poems To Read In The Rain

I am not the woman you wish me to be
Sweet and silent as the morning breeze
A pleasant kiss upon your cheek
Barely brushing the autumn leaves

No.

I am the rush of howling wind
Too wild and free to hold your hand
A magnificent storm of chaotic thoughts
Raining arrows, piercing hearts

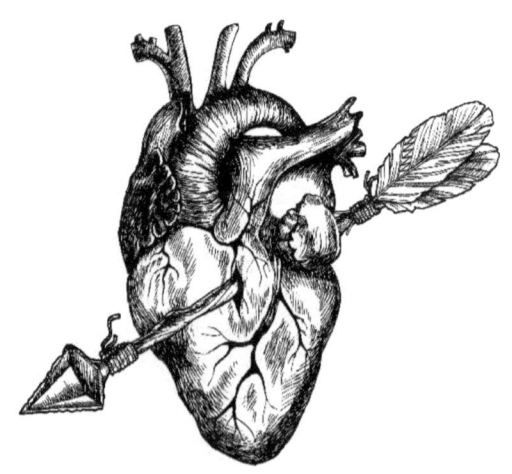

Jennifer Gordon

Always she has felt this wild
She was born a full moon child
Reflecting all chaotic light
Shining best on blackest nights

They will love you the most
When you are still and silent
But believe me when I say
You were made to roar
With the lions

Jennifer Gordon

Here's to all the wild ones
Covered in scars, adorned in red
The rebels, the beautiful disasters
With reckless souls that long to be fed
The lovers, the listeners
The muses born to be free
Here's to the ones who know me well,
Who cherish the secrets they'll never tell

He asked me once:
What are you made of?
Your warmth feels like fire,
Your whispers speak
In tongues I can't define
Your spirit an enigma
Of the rarest kind
My heart is desperate
In your hands, begging
To know the ending
Am I to be saved, or devoured?
Are you an angel, or a vulture?

Yes.

Jennifer Gordon

His smile is a pirate of guilty pleasures
My heart, a mermaid in sensual waters
But I long to be like ocean waves
Dancing in rhythm beneath the moon
Declaring my presence upon the shore
And drowning pirates in the storm

Poems To Read In The Rain

She is a puzzle of a million pieces
A mystery often sought
But never solved
Seen in sections
Understood only in parts
A masterpiece of fractured art

Jennifer Gordon

If you wake one day
To find I haven't stayed
Please, just let me be
Let me run, aching for the sun
For I am at the mercy
Of an untamed heart
Longing only to be free

Poems To Read In The Rain

I was not designed for the nine to five
For the mundane drones of normal life
My feral heart craves days that sway
In tune with the rhythm of falling rain

Jennifer Gordon

This world declares an abundance of hollow words
Lifeless utterances that pass for wisdom
Self righteous, fame seeking speeches
Everywhere, a hum of brilliantly crafted nothingness
Give me instead the words dripping blood
Scraping the throat as they're screamed out loud
Filled with the breath of a thousand lungs
Meaning life to their speakers' tongues

Poems To Read In The Rain

I shall not succumb
To the numbness of complacency
The lull of monotony
Nor the cadence of a simple life
I will own my demons
And turn them to dragons
Sing to the ashes
And dance in the madness
I will decide to be alive
One breathtaking sunrise at a time

Jennifer Gordon

Her soul was carved from ancient stone
Old as the earth, vast as the moon
Wild as the flowers caressing the breeze
Deep as the endless ocean
Causing tidal waves with reckless ease

Poems To Read In The Rain

When you are old, worn and gray
I pray you remember being carried away
Lost in moments that arose like fire
Immersed in the pain of love expired
Meek beneath a boundless sky
Paramount in your children's eyes
I hope your limbs are awake and weary
Aching from all those years of living
I wish you a phase of peaceful days
Recalling the ways you danced in the rain

Jennifer Gordon

My spirit wanders
In curious contentment
Like petals blown
From wildflowers
Breaking free
Of their foundation
Floating towards
A path less taken

Poems To Read In The Rain

My mind is a humble, foreign land
Built of verses on crooked paths
A wilderness of tainted trees
Shifting and swaying in a worldly breeze
A haze of rich, unfiltered light
Creeping through cracks of jagged writes
A terrain of pillaged disarray
Foraged of thoughts which wits replace
Herein lie the quiet cries
Of private pages soaked in disguise
Rugged edges, supple swells
Wanderlust in a washed up shell

Jennifer Gordon

Chapter 4:
Nature Loves Back

Poems To Read In The Rain

Jennifer Gordon

This morning I went to church in the woods
Approached my sanctuary in solitude
Inhaled the pines into my lungs
Placed my palms upon their trunks
Considered the richness of their roots
How beautiful,
To be so densely connected to the earth
To know the depth of your own worth
The sun was low in the eastern sky
Barely visible through the trees
Revealing only slivers of herself to me
My skin was warmed by her subtle touch
A kindred embrace from the world above
I closed my eyes, feeling the breeze upon my lashes
Here at home with my feet in the dirt
My heart felt a peace unique to this place
And in my chest arose a swell
Of something resembling that word called love

Poems To Read In The Rain

I have always believed that God built me
Out of twigs and weeds and fragile things
For I have ever felt small amidst the trees
The way they sway in tune with the breeze
With roots that weave into the earth
Joining themselves to the heart of her
How their signs of aging are viewed as beauty
Their purpose essential as the air we breathe
The strength it takes to withstand the storm
Able to bend yet again without breaking
Lose the colors that adorn them
Each and every year without complaining
Surely I am made of less than these
At best, I am a humble pile of fallen leaves
Collected and sheltered in the forest eaves

Jennifer Gordon

All my life
I have cherished the storm
For she understands my soul
And my spirit loves to sing along
As wild thunder roars

Poems To Read In The Rain

The woods have a way of seducing my soul
Inducing my heart with primal rhythms
Aligning beats of my chest with steps on the path
Immersing my mind in the slowness of time

There is wisdom buried beneath the soil
Stories the earth has cherished in her breast
Histories of afflictions unknown, untold
Lurking in layers below the surface

I long to know her secrets
And so I let my spirit float
Weaving a wandering trail
Through a fog of wordless ghosts

Perhaps if I linger long enough
She will embrace my foreign shape
Absorb my bones into the pulse of forest tones
Share with me the things she knows

Jennifer Gordon

There is magic in the midnight sky
Rich with darkness, adorned in light
Magnetic energy in the rushing waters
Flowing free and fierce beneath the sun
Strength in the stones, lending balance
To the softness of sand upon the shores
Beauty in the ever changing lakes
The depth of the forest and all its secrets
This earth is mine and I am hers
She speaks to me in mystic tongues

Poems To Read In The Rain

I have never been able to embrace the city lights
The chaos of crowded concrete on a summer night
Lost in a haze of industrious fog
Where all I long for is a hint of clarity
Where separation from the roots of the earth
Is a sign of prosperity
How could my heart feel warmth in a place
Where the songs of birds are never heard?
Where my feet can never find the dirt?
Give me instead the freezing streams
That trickle down from mountain peaks
The mud upon my humble hands
Left by hours of exploring the land
Give me raw, give me wild
Give me blankets of stars kissed in the night
By the love I breathe and the words I write

At dawn I arise with the red summer sun
Sprinkle intimate thoughts of you
Upon the mist of the morning air
Watch them float on cotton clouds
Into the blue, light and free
I lay my limbs on flower beds
Melt upon their softened stems
Let the daylight pass me by
And await the sparrows with your reply

Poems To Read In The Rain

Embers of the summer sun
Fade quietly
Down beneath the shadows of the earth
Here she sleeps
Replaced by the harvest moon

The echo of your voice
Latched onto the breeze
Clung as it weaved
Danced delicately
Among the wilted autumn leaves
It reached me there
On the forest floor
Tracing shadows through my hair
It hovered softly on my chest
Begged my breath to breathe it in
Filled my lungs
With whispered words
Light as feathers
Free as birds

Golden, as in the essence of first morning light
As the sun breaches the horizon
And her complexion touches softly down
Upon the earth
Golden, as in the sand within the shallows
Thick beneath the mirrored sea,
Illuminated just enough
By the colored sky of a warming day
Golden, as in the eyes of eagles in flight
As they soar in splendor above the river's offerings
Of quenching flow and hunted catch
Golden, as in the endless fields of wheat
Swaying in tune to the silent melody
Of the faithful evening breeze
Golden, as in my love for intimate views
An ever present hue
The rays of me that follow you

Jennifer Gordon

Oh to be a flame
In the night
Releasing heat
In gust and waves
Feeding the wind
With magic light

Poems To Read In The Rain

On the days when life is harder than most
I seek my solace close to home
Trek to the edge of our cherished land
Strip myself of weighted plans
Naked of constraints
I lay my body upon the earth
Spill heavy thoughts into the dirt
Refill my mind with the songs of birds

Drop me here and leave me be
Let my spirit wander free
This forest floor
Is but a cushion for my soul
And the mountain winds
Shall caress my cheeks
For I was born to live and breathe
Among the pines and jagged peaks

Poems To Read In The Rain

I was born in the season of spring
How fitting
That I should enter the world as it's being reborn
Surrounded by a hum of new beginnings
Seedlings, flightless wings and other innocent things
Things like me

Summer brought out the child in me
Lazy days, wild and free
Even then I had an anxious soul
Always searching for places to roam
Life was kind, the winds were calm
Burdens just light enough for hands so small

In autumn I bloomed a brilliant red
A fire in my lungs filled the air with smoke
As I floated between the burning leaves
Blending in with the changing trees
I soaked this season in through my pores
Let it flow through my veins as a river of warmth

But the chill in the air became bitter cold
Winter blew in, settled deep in my bones
The vibrance of the world slowly shriveled away
The skies turned gray, all faded shades
No growth, no life, no phantom faith
Somehow becoming both dead and alive

Seasons come and seasons go
At least that's what they like to say
What do I know?
I'm just a woman
Buried in snow
Dreaming of a spring they promise will come

Poems To Read In The Rain

Deep in barren woods was she
A wayward lonesome soul
Perched upon a toppled tree
Weeping shattered dreams
Into the fallen snow

Jennifer Gordon

Early morning mist
Amidst a gentle breeze
Flows in graceful waves
Upon my moistened skin
Air lightly kissed
With winter's frosted lips
Renews fresh breath
Within my withered lungs
Here I listen for her song
The lonely bird
Who waited too long
To travel south
With feathered flocks
My presence now her warmth
Her beauty to me
A beacon of hope
A natural reminder
That the signs of seasons overlap
Though the burdens
Of the world hold fast
She and I will weather this cold
Breathe in the somber chill
Releasing back into the wind
A sweetened song of strength
As long as our lungs are able

Poems To Read In The Rain

Some days I envy the fallen leaves
Their work is finished, their effort spent
No one expects them to reattach

Jennifer Gordon

I see you in the dawn of sunlight
In the rays that dance with birds in flight
I see you in the steam that rises
From the warmth of coffee upon my lips
As I gaze in awe of the horizon
I feel you here beside my skin
Inside three words I whisper again
Within the spaces between my ribs
And in the embrace I yearn to give

Poems To Read In The Rain

Alone I ponder the birds of the air
How fearless they appear
Soaring through the wayward wind
Knowing they'll find a way back again
Instinctual hearts direct their course
No fear of love, loss, or remorse
How I long to immerse my bones
Inside their feathers and call it home
To freely float amidst the sky
And truly live while I'm alive

Jennifer Gordon

My spirit longs to hold the earth
To lace my fingers through her dirt
Feel the rawness of nature on my skin
Be close to something real again
Breathe her scent of wild pines
Fill my lungs with precious time
Relish the stillness within my chest
In solitude on a forest path
Give me the music of mountain streams
The complexity of ancient trees
This is nourishment for my soul
Finding myself in the depth of it all

This morning I awoke
With magnets in my chest
Muscles straining with unrest
The pull of my wounds
Towards the wide open blue
Pricks of longing
Inching their way along my limbs
Drawing freckled arrows
Patterns of risk for my will to follow
Days like this I am ripe with desire
For jumping rivers and starting fires
For running wild with the wolves
Screaming life into my veins
And carving the courage of my name
Into the flesh of darkest woods

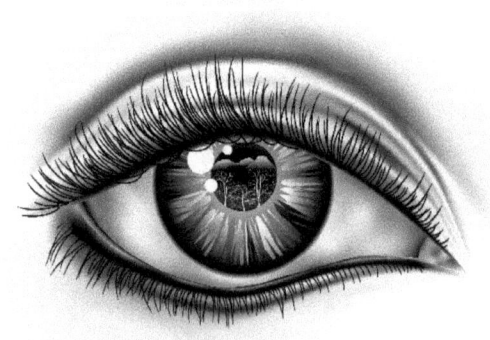

Jennifer Gordon

To reach for the stars is a meaningless task
Trust me, dear those dreams never last
Instead aim wide for the blue black sky
A canvas adorned with movement and life
For the stars will die and fall away
But never the sky, endless of days

Poems To Read In The Rain

Sometimes I wonder where I'll be
The night I take my final breaths
I hope I'm somewhere wild and free
Smiling wide at the scent of death
Gazing in awe of a million stars
And I pray I'm not wondering where you are
That you will be there by my side
Beneath the moon, hand in mine

Jennifer Gordon

Poems To Read In The Rain

This book is dedicated to the distance
Which stretches from the ocean floor
To the stars adorning heaven's door

Jennifer Gordon

Poems To Read In The Rain

www.ingramcontent.com/pod-product-compliance
Lightning Source LLC
Chambersburg PA
CBHW070447050426
42451CB00015B/3379